Little Bub!

For Kora!

By Jahri Jah Jah!

www.jjj.co.nz

Self published by Shane Rosemeyer
Takaka, New Zealand
ISBN 978-0-9864669-7-7

I0177975

Baby
Pēpē

Mum

Whaea / Māmā

Dad
Maṯua / Pāpā

Bottle
Pātara

Banana
Panana

Apple
Āporo

Potty

Pō mimi

Teddy Bear

Teti pea

Flower

Putiputi

Car
Motokā

Sheep

Hipi

Cow

Kau

Bee
PT

Bird
Manu

Butterfly
Pūrerehua

Food
Kai

Spoon
Pūnu

Cuddle
Awhiawhi

Kiwi
Kiwi

Moon
Marama

Sun
Rā

Cat

Ngeru

Dog
Kurī

House
Whare

Fish

Ika

More cool books
By Jahri Jah Jah!

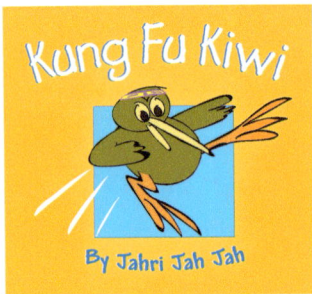

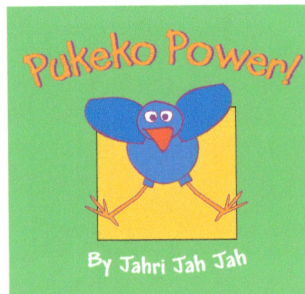

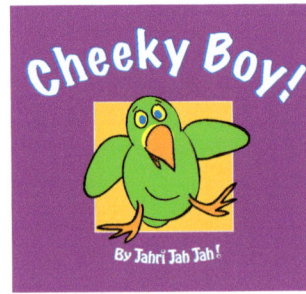

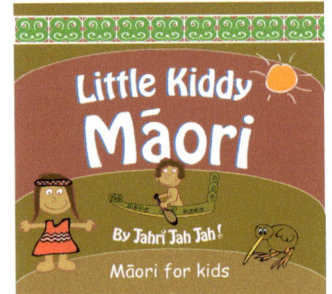

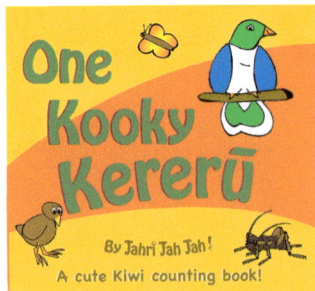

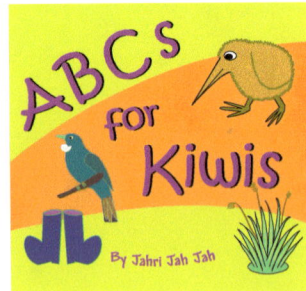

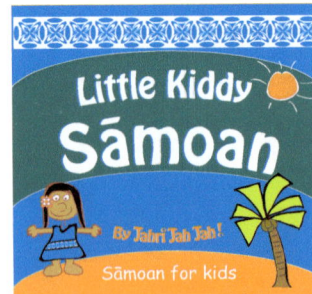

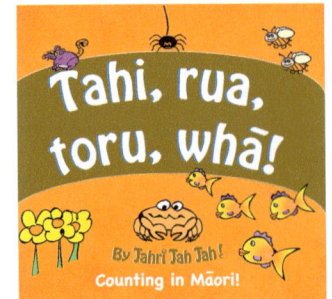

Kung Fu Kiwi
By Jahri Jah Jah

Pukeko Power!
By Jahri Jah Jah

Cheeky Boy!
By Jahri Jah Jah!

Little Kiddy Māori
By Jahri Jah Jah!
Māori for kids

One Kooky Kererū
By Jahri Jah Jah!
A cute Kiwi counting book!

ABCs for Kiwis
By Jahri Jah Jah

Little Kiddy Sāmoan
By Jahri Jah Jah!
Sāmoan for kids

Tahi, rua, toru, whā!
By Jahri Jah Jah!
Counting in Māori!

www.ingramcontent.com/pod-product-compliance
Lightning Source LLC
Chambersburg PA
CBHW040023050426
42452CB00002B/108